Magical Mantras

&

Sacred Sounds

Awaken Your Higher Self: The Power of Chanting

Contents

Introduction 4
Chapter 1 – The Origin Of Mantras 6
    So what makes them so powerful? 7
Chapter 2 – The Art of Chanting? 11
    Cultivate a Stable Mindset 12
    Assume a Comfortable Position 13
    Learn to Release Tension 13
    Cultivating Your Mantras 14
    The Essence Beyond Counting 15
    Embrace the Journey 16
Chapter 3 – Chanting Your First Mantra 17
Chapter 4 – Mantras To Attain Positive Energy 22
    Seed Mantra 22
    Rama Mantra 23
    Vishnu Mantra 24
    Shanti Mantra 25
    Gayatri Mantra 27
Chapter 5 – Mantras For Good Health & Being 30
    Aham Arorgyam 30
    Sun Mantra 33
    Shivaya Mantra 35
    Dhanvantri Mantra 36
    Mahamrityunjaya Mantra 38
Chapter 6 – Mantras For Wealth & Prosperity 40

Ganesha Mantra 40

Lokah Samastah Mantra 41

Lakshmi Mantra 42

Padma Lakshmi Mantra 44

Kuber Mantra 45

Kuber Lakshmi Mantras 46

Chapter 7 – Mantras To Attain Peace & Tranquility 49

Durga Mantra 49

Kama Deva Mantra 51

Pavamana Mantra 52

Vaastupurushaaya Mantra 53

Brahma Mantra 55

Conclusion 57

Introduction

How well do you truly know yourself?

In this vast universe, we all exist like a drop in an ocean. As humans, we can either wither in anonymity or strive for excellence. Every day, every moment, we make this choice. The series of decisions that you have made in your life has led you right here – to this very moment.

Now, another choice beckons. You can either continue to drift through life, remaining a mere spectator as the world unfolds, or you can choose to reach out, to forge a connection with the universe. After all, we are all woven from the same stardust, each of us a unique fragment of the cosmos.

Embark on a transformative journey with us, exploring the resonant power of mantras and sacred sounds, ancient tools of healing and empowerment still embraced by millions across the globe. Mantras, integral to the spiritual fabric of Hinduism, are not just sounds; they are vessels of energy, capable of bringing peace, healing, and a profound connection to the cosmos.

Science, too, acknowledges the power of sound, affirming that specific sound waves can soothe the senses, harmonize the mind and body, and unlock realms of untapped potential. This guide is your gateway to the mystical world of mantras, a journey to discover the divine symphony of the universe.

We have handpicked some of the most powerful mantras from Hinduism to help you attain a perfect balance in your life. From health to mental strength, and happiness to prosperity, with the help of these divine sounds you can attain it all. Take a deep breath and commence this amazing journey with us!

Chapter 1 – The Origin Of Mantras

Mantras consist of a phrase, a word, or even a sound that is repeated in a rhythmic manner. They are often referred to as "sacred sounds," serving as a tool to aid individuals in meditation. Originating from Hinduism, mantras are considered to embody sacred syllables, representing the profound spiritual truths and divine energies.

Hinduism, one of the world's oldest religions, originated between 1500-3000 BC and is currently embraced by over a billion people, making it the third-largest religion globally. It offers a vast array of spiritual tools and practices, among which mantras hold a special place, being a medium to connect with the divine.

Mantras have been integral to Hinduism since its inception. Typically, mantras are phrases in Sanskrit—the language of the Hindu Vedas and other sacred texts—that encapsulate a certain essence and vibration. They are believed to have a transformative power, altering one's consciousness, and bringing about spiritual awakening and healing.

A mantra might consist of a single word, like "Om," or span several lines, narrating a story. Originally, they were composed to praise the universe, a specific Hindu deity or element, or to depict a natural wonder. Each mantra is said to have its unique vibrational frequency, resonating with different aspects of the universe and the human psyche.

Regardless of which sacred mantra one chooses to chant, all mantras have the power to penetrate to one's core. They can act as a key to unlock true potential, transcending the everyday mundane state and guiding individuals on the path to self-righteousness. By regularly practicing mantra meditation, individuals can experience a deeper sense of peace, enhanced focus, and a heightened state of awareness, ultimately leading to self-realization and enlightenment.

So what makes them so powerful?

What indeed makes mantras so potent? One of the many facets that render the chanting of mantras unique is that the practice does not require adherence to a specific religion or God. It is predominantly about the sound produced by chanting these sacred syllables that holds paramount significance. Chanting allows one to contemplate their inner thoughts and feelings, promoting self-reflection, introspection as opposed to blindly following the group. This characteristic is a primary reason why Hinduism is often perceived more as a philosophy or way of life than a structured religion.

While the ancient values of mantras and their significance in religions like Hinduism and Buddhism might be well-known, the scientific rationale behind chanting may be less familiar. Take, for example, the chanting of the word "Om" (A-u-m), revered as one of the most pure and sacred sounds.

When chanted sequentially and rhythmically, "Om" induces vibrations throughout the entire body. Scientific studies have documented the generation of unique patterns of activity in the spine, brain, abdomen, waist, and other major body regions during its chanting. One can perceive the ascent of energy from the abdominal area to the brain, with the energy being conveyed via the spine.

Regular practice in mantra chanting can facilitate the attainment of optimal harmony in one's life and can significantly enhance cognitive functions. In groundbreaking research, findings have revealed that the practice of chanting mantras can enhance proficiency in mathematics and analytical thinking. The rhythmic recitation of these sacred sounds can markedly amplify concentration levels and serve as a powerful antidote to stress, promoting mental tranquility and balance.

It goes without saying that by merely reciting a few sacred mantras, one can cultivate a positive ambiance and achieve a harmonious balance in life. The act of chanting can harmonize the body, mind, and spirit, fostering a deeper, more profound connection with the universe. This is not merely a claim made by numerous gurus and yogis but is also substantiated by various scientific studies.

Now that you are acquainted with the transformative power of mantras, let's proceed to explore how to chant your inaugural mantra.

Chapter 2 – The Art of Chanting?

Mantras can wield transformative power, shaping the contours of your life in profound ways. However, before embarking on this spiritual odyssey and attaining spiritual contentment, it is crucial to approach it correctly. Many novices, unfamiliar with the essence of mantras, hastily choose one and begin chanting without preparing their minds, a common pitfall.

Chanting is an intricate art, requiring time and patience to master. Fear not! We are here to guide you. By chanting mantras correctly, you can seamlessly integrate meditation into your life and evolve over time. Embrace this journey step by step, preparing yourself to chant your first mantra.

Just like a child learning to walk, mastering the art of chanting and meditation requires perseverance and resilience. A child, when first attempting to walk, stumbles and falls numerous times. However, it is through these falls that the child learns, gets up again, and eventually, walking becomes second nature to them. Similarly, the journey of chanting and meditation is filled with metaphorical falls and stumbles. It might feel unnatural or challenging initially, but with consistent practice and unwavering dedication, it becomes a natural and integral part of one's daily routine.

In this spiritual journey, every stumble is a step forward, every moment of struggle is a building block towards mastery. It's about cultivating patience, refining focus, and learning to synchronize the mind, body, and spirit in a harmonious rhythm. The initial challenges faced are but stepping stones leading to a path of inner peace, heightened awareness, and profound spiritual awakening. So, approach this practice with an open heart and a resilient spirit, allowing the transformative power of mantras to guide you to your true self.

Cultivate a Stable Mindset

To commence this journey, you need to be open to new ideas. Embrace new perspectives and most importantly believe in the transformative power of divine sounds. Find a serene spot, free from distractions, including electronic devices, to recite mantras. Avoid crowded places initially, seeking solitude in a quiet room or a peaceful outdoor setting.

Assume a Comfortable Position

Your posture is pivotal while chanting. A relaxed yet alert posture, such as the lotus position, is recommended, ensuring your spine is straight and your core engaged. However, comfort is key, so find a position that suits you, using support if needed.

Learn to Release Tension

We won't lie – it's not an easy task to relax. Relaxation might seem elusive initially, but with practice, it becomes second nature. Don't focus on your past or your future. Instead, think of the present moment.

Breathe in and breathe out while concentrating on your body. Slowly close your eyes and while inhaling deeply, focus on your forehead and gradually move to your eyes. Follow this and relax your muscles as you focus on your back, shoulders, arms, legs, and so on. With your eyes closed, visualize serene landscapes or count breaths to aid relaxation, releasing tension from each part of your body.

Cultivating Your Mantras

Mantras come in various forms, each resonating with different aspects of life such as health, healing, mental stability, and wealth. Begin your journey with a simple mantra, allowing its vibrations to gently introduce you to this ancient practice. We will delve deeper into the myriad of mantras available as we progress through this guide.

It is crucial to focus on pronunciation. Before immersing yourself in the chanting, strive to understand the correct pronunciation and the inherent meaning of each mantra. Creating sacred sound is the essence of chanting, and correct articulation is important. By focusing on pronunciation, you can deepen your connection to the mantra and enhance its transformative power.

Consider the mantra "Om," a universal sound representing the essence of the universe. Incorrect pronunciation can alter its vibrations and, consequently, its impact. So, take your time to learn, to listen, and to pronounce it correctly, allowing its sacred vibrations to resonate within you.

The Essence Beyond Counting

Contrary to popular belief, obsessing over the count of your chants can detract from the essence of the experience. A rosary or japa mala can aid in maintaining count without diverting your focus. Using such aids is not mandatory but can significantly enhance your chanting experience.

In Hindu tradition, there is no stringent rule regarding the number of chants, but chanting 11, 21, 51, 101, or 108 times is highly recommended. A traditional Hindu japa mala, adorned with 108 beads, can simplify this process for you, allowing you to immerse in the chant without the burden of counting.

Embrace the Journey

You're on the brink of a transformative journey. Avoid mechanical, forced chanting; it will lead you nowhere. Be natural, be yourself, and sometimes, surrender to the universe and let it steer your path.

Approach chanting with a pure and open heart, allowing the divine vibrations to guide you to enlightenment. Now, with an open heart and a receptive mind, let's introduce you to your first mantra.

Chapter 3 – Chanting Your First Mantra

Let's practice your first mantra – "*Om*."

It is the simplest of all mantras and is ideally used in almost every kind of chanting. Most of the people start chanting with this simple yet efficient mantra, which represents the sound of the universe. Yes, according to the Hindu Mythology, it is the same sound which is produced by the vibration of the universe.

Okay! Now, this would be a little tricky. You need to pronounce *Om* not from your tongue but from your epiglottis. It should come from within your core. Its correct pronunciation is "A-u-m."

It would sound similar to that of "ome" in home. Ideally, Om is made of four sounds – a, u, m, and the silence.

While chanting, you need to make sure that you focus on every sound. It should be chanted as "Ooommm" to be precise in a rhythmic manner. While you chant, you can feel your epiglottis vibrating at the frequency of the universe. Go ahead! Give it a try.

Great! Now let's make you take a perfect lotus position. Start by sitting on a mat (or a blanket) while keeping your spine straight. Now, bend your right towards your chest in such a way that your right foot should be up and resting on the opposite side.

Gradually, bend your left knee as well, making your ankle rest on the opposite shin. Its bottom would also be facing the ceiling or the sky. Make sure that you bring your knees as closely as possible while keeping your spine straight.

Inhale a little and lose your shoulders while resting your hands on your knees. With your palms facing up, join your thumb with your index figure. This would make an "o" in between. This is also known as *"Gyan mudra"* or the wisdom seal. Extend every other finger while exhaling.

After assuming lotus position, a posture symbolic of purity and enlightenment, take several deep, slow breaths. Close your eyes and open your mind to the wisdom of the universe, allowing the cosmic energies to infuse your being. Once you feel ready, clearly, and loudly recite "Om" at least three times, allowing all other thoughts to fade away, immersing yourself in the sacred vibrations of the universe.

Focus on each sound, breaking it down and pausing between each mantra. When you pause, it's like having a blank canvas. The vibrations from the mantra can then paint a beautiful picture in your mind. It's like creating a one-of-a-kind masterpiece in your soul. Imagine the mantra as a ball of energy. It starts in your heart and grows bigger and bigger until it surrounds your whole body. The light from the mantra fills you up and makes you feel clean and pure. This visualization makes the mantra more powerful and helps you connect with the divine.

Acknowledging the silence between each mantra is crucial, as it allows the sound vibrations to resonate within you, creating ripples of positive energy throughout your being. Continue to breathe calmly and serenely, chanting this powerful mantra for another 5 minutes.

As you chant the mantra, you may feel vibrations resonating through your body. It's like the universe is dancing inside of you. Gradually, you'll feel yourself rising above the everyday things that stress you out. You'll enter a place of peace and heightened awareness. This is a journey beyond the ordinary, a voyage to the very essence of existence. When you feel ready, stop chanting but keep breathing. Stay connected to the universal energies.

After you finish chanting, take a few deep breaths, and slowly open your eyes. Keep your hands in the wisdom seal. Tilt your head slightly towards the sky. This is a gesture of reverence and openness to the divine energies. Hold this position for a few moments, then return your head to the center.

Visualize the divine energies flowing down from the sky, entering your body through the crown of your head. Feel these energies filling your body with peace, love, and light.

Release your fingers and gently place your hands on your temples, massaging softly. This gentle massage is like a soothing balm, allowing your mind to integrate the profound experiences of your chant. You may feel your brain processing and realigning, returning to its natural state of balance and harmony.

Congratulations! You have successfully completed your first chant. This is not just a step, but a leap towards spiritual awakening and self-discovery. Now, let's explore some other significant mantras from Hindu mythology, each a gem of spiritual wisdom, guiding you on your path to enlightenment.

Chapter 4 – Mantras To Attain Positive Energy

We all are driven by the energy we get from the universe. No one likes to be surrounded with negativity as it can cause unwanted stress and even led to depression. With the help of sacred sounds, you can break this pattern and attain a positive environment around you.

Let's start by exploring various mantras that can help you unblock energy and diminish negative energy from your life. Mantras can indeed help you attain an optimistic approach in your life. Start chanting these ancient mantras and we are sure you would see a difference in your life soon.

Seed Mantra

The seed (or *bija*) mantra is one of the core mantras that can help you attract positive energy by making you the center of your own universe. It has five distinctive sounds and can be recited while sitting in an ideal lotus position. Just breathe in and chant this sacred mantra at least 11 or 51 times in the beginning.

Mantra: *Om Krim Shrim Hrim Hum*

Pronunciation: *Aum K-reem Sh-reem H-reem H-oom*

Every sound has a peculiar meaning. *Om* will help you gather energy from your body while *Krim* will commence the purification process. Subsequently, *Shrim* will bring happiness and contentment in your life and *Hrim* will awaken your creative soul. Lastly, *Hum* will heal your soul and spread a positive aura, both around and within.

Rama Mantra

This mantra is dedicated to Lord Rama, who was an incarnation of Lord Vishnu. In Hindu mythology, the three major gods are Lord Vishnu, Lord Brahma, and Lord Shiva. Each one plays a distinctive role of being a generator, an operator, and a destroyer. Most of the mantras in Hindu mythologies are associated with various deities.

The Rama Mantra praises the power of Lord Rama and can help you attain positivity and prosperity in your life.

Mantra: *Om Ram Ramaya Namaha*

Pronunciation: *Aum Raam Raam-aaya Naa-ma-ha*

It is associated with our solar chakra and enables the inflow of healing energy from our atmosphere to our body and mind. It translates to "Let Lord Rama's perfection exists in all of us."

Chanting this Sanskrit mantra will help you attain a perfect balance in your life and would heal your tired mind and soul.

Vishnu Mantra

Just like the Rama Mantra is associated with Lord Rama, the Vishnu Mantra will help you preach Lord Vishnu in all his glory. According to the Hindu Mythology, Lord Vishnu is not only the creator of the universe, but the whole universe is, in fact, a part of his divine spirit.

It has been assumed that if you chant the Vishnu Mantra with a sincere heart, then you can fulfill every desire of yours. Not only will it bring happiness and prosperity in your life, but would help you break free from stress as well.

Mantra: Om Namo Bhagavate Vasudevaya Namaha

Pronunciation: Aum Na-moh Bhaag-waa-teh Vaasu-dev-ayah Naa-ma-ha

The mantra will deliver goodness in your life and will certainly bring you a little closer to the universe. It is also considered as one of the most powerful hymns in the Hindu mythology. It can also give you immense power to overcome an obstacle.

Shanti Mantra

"Shanti" literally translates to "peace" in Sanskrit. The regular chanting of this mantra can help you attain a sense of peace and contentment in your life. It will help you attract a sense of serenity and would make you feel calm and relaxed. The mantra doesn't preach any god or goddess directly but is rather focused on attaining a non-violent approach that we should all have towards life.

Mantra: *Om Shanti Shanti Shanti*

Pronunciation: *Aum Sha-an-ti Sha-an-ti Sha-an-ti*

It literally translates to "Let there be peace."

When you are chanting the word "Shanti", you need to close your eyes and simply let go of yourself. The pitch of the first "Shanti" word should be greater. Gradually, decrease your pitch while repeating the same word. The third "Shanti" word should be followed by silence before repeating the chant once again.

Gayatri Mantra

Gayatri Mantra is often known as "the universal prayer" and is considered as the most important mantra in Hinduism. It has been originated from the Rigveda and is dedicated to the power of the universe itself. It has also been used in various other holy books like the *Manusmriti* and the *Bhagwada Gita*.

The hymn has four distinctive parts. Let's unravel them one by one.

Mantra: *Om Bhūr Bhuvaḥ Svaḥ*

Tát Savitúr Váreṇ(i)yaṃ

Bhárgo Devásya Dhīmahi

Dhíyo Yó Naḥ Prachodayāt

Pronunciation: *Aum Bhoor Bhuvaha Ssuwaha*

Tah-at saa-vee-taar Vaa-re-ni-yaam

Bhaar-goh Dev-aasya Dhee-mahi

Dhi-yoh Yoh Na-ah Prah-cho-da-yah-at

It was in 1807, when Sir William Jones translated the mantra as "Let us adore the supremacy of that divine sun, the god-head who illuminates all, who recreates all, from whom all proceed, to whom all must return, whom we invoke to direct our understandings aright in our progress toward his holy seat."

The mantra is directly linked to the power of the sun and will help you bring the positivity of the sun to your holy seat. Try to start meditating by reciting the Gayatri Mantra in the beginning. One of the best ways to chant it is by sitting under the luminous light of the sun and preaching its divine power with the assistance of its sacred sound.

Practice these thoughtful and powerful mantras to bring a sense of optimism in your life. If you are suffering from any unwanted stress or are being surrounded by negativity in your workplace or life in general, then these mantras would certainly bring a breath of fresh air to your life.

After attaining a positive attitude, focus on your health. In the next section, we will make you familiar with some productive mantras that can help you heal your body and attain a healthy lifestyle.

Chapter 5 – Mantras For Good Health & Being

The usage of mantras to attain good health is not an uncommon one. The practitioners of Hinduism and Buddhism have been using mantras not only to heal themselves, but also to attain a healthy mind and body. It is also associated with the principle of *Reiki*, which is the practice of healing by the power of touch and sound.

With the flow of energy, you can certainly strengthen your senses and attain a healthy lifestyle. Just like most of the other mantras, they should also be chanted while sitting in the lotus position.

Aham Arorgyam

The "Aham Arogyam" hymn is considered as one of the most powerful mantras that can help you to heal yourself and to boost your health as well. The Sanskrit hymn is usually narrated by those who would like to remain healthy or would like to cure a persisting disease.

Mantra: *Aham Arogyam*

Aham Anandam

Aham Madhura

Aham Purnam

Aham Mrityunjai

Aham Swatantra

Aham Ahinsa

Pronunciation: *Aa-ham Aa-roh-ga-yam*

Aa-ham AA-nan-dam

Aa-ham Maa-duh-oorah

Aa-ham Poor-naam

Aa-ham M-rie-t-yun-jai

Aa-ham Swa-taan-tra

Aa-ham Aa-heen-sah

The literal meaning of the mantra is as follows:

Aham Arogyam – I'm free from every disease

Aham Anandam – I'm in a surreal bliss

Aham Madhura – I'm enjoying the nectar of life

Aham Purnam – I'm complete and close to perfection

Aham Mrityunjai – I'm free from the cycle of life and death

Aham Swatantra – I'm independent and can't be tamed

Aham Ahinsa – I'm peaceful and non-violent

Just like the meaning of this thoughtful mantra, it can help you cure every disease and liberate you from the vicious circle of life and death.

Sun Mantra

There are plenty of mantras that are directly connected to the sun in the Hindu mythology. The sun holds a significant place in the religious practice, as out of all the deities, it is one of the most powerful gods that can be seen by humans. By chanting the mantra of the sun during sunrise, you can empower yourself with its high energy.

In Vedic culture, the sun holds the power to give light, positive energy, and prosperity in our life. Additionally, it has been observed that by chanting this mantra, you can overcome your respiratory troubles and empower the kind of energy that would last all day long.

Mantra: *Om Hrim Sum Suryaya Namah*

Pronunciation: *Aum Hreem Summ Soor-aya-yah Naa-mah*

The mantra praises the power of the sun and requests the deity to empower our body with his resonating power. It has plenty of other versions also, including the famous "*Om ghrinih suraya namah*" or the longer hymn of "*Om hram hrim hraum sah suryaya namah.*"

If you are specifically struggling with anxiety, stress or negative thinking, then chant this mantra 108 times during the sunrise. You will likely experience a substantial improvement in your energy levels and focus.

Shivaya Mantra

As stated, Lord Shiva is one of the three primary deities in the Hindu mythology. He is known as the God of death and destruction. If you like to attain a long and happy life, then you should definitely chant this famous mantra. It is considered as one of the most powerful mantras in Hinduism and holds the power to eradicate even the deadliest of diseases. It can certainly help you live a long and healthy life.

Mantra: Om Namah Shivaya

Pronunciation: Aum Na-ma-ha Shi-va-yah

It is one of the most famous mantras in the world and chances are that you must have already heard of it. Practice this by closing your eyes and while focusing on every part of your body, since the mantra can heal your physical, psychological, and spiritual flaws.

According to the Hindu mythology, there is a part of Vishnu, Brahma, and Shivaya in all of us. The mantra literally translates to "I bow to the inner self."

 Of course, when you say "Shivaya", it implies that you are bowing to the deity, but according to *Shivaism*, you are bowing to the part of *Shivaya* that resides in your inner self. This is what makes this mantra so effective and thoughtful.

Dhanvantri Mantra

The Dhanvantri mantra is one of the most powerful mantras dedicated to Lord Vishnu. If you are suffering from any disease or illness, then you should definitely try chanting this as much as you can. It can liberate you from every kind of ailment or suffering. Though, before you start chanting this mantra, you need to visualize your suffering or disease.

You need to make yourself believe that you are going to fight the illness and would attain a healthy mind and body. You need to assure yourself of a better tomorrow and should be filled with optimism while chanting this mantra. Don't chant it with a need, but as if you are already grateful for experiencing this amazing journey.

Mantra: Om Namo Bhagavate Maha Sudarshanaya Vasudevaya Dhanvantaraye

Amrita Kalasha Hastaya, Sarvabhaya Vinashaya, Sarvaroga Nivaranaya

Trilokya Pataye, Trilokya Nidhaye

Shri Maha Vishnu Swaroopa, Shri Dhanvatri Swaroopa,

Shri Shri Shri Aushadha Chakra Narayanaya Swaha.

Pronunciation: Aum Bhaag-wateh Ma-ha Su-dar-shaa-nayah Vaa-su-de-vayah Dhan-van-ta-ra-yeh

Aam-rita Ka-la-shah Has-ta-ya, Sar-va-bha-yah Vi-na-sha-yah Ni-va-ra-na-yah

T-ree-law-k-yah pah-ta-yah, T-ree-law-k-yah Ni-dha-yah

Shree Ma-ha Vish-nu S-wah-roo-pah, Shree Dhan-van-ta-ra-yeh S-wah-roo-pah,

Shree Shree Shree Aaw-shah-dha Chaa-kra Naa-raa-ya-na-ya S-wa-hah

Lord Vishnu is often depicted in his original form, holding a pot. It is considered that his pot holds the nectar of immortality. In this mantra, you would be praying the Lord Vishnu, not only to provide a long and healthy life, but also to take away every kind of illness and suffering from your life as well.

Mahamrityunjaya Mantra

Mahamrityunjaya Mantra is considered as one of the oldest mantras in Hinduism and has been taken from the Rigveda. It is also known as a "life-giving" or a "death-conquering mantra" by many devotees as it can help one avoid the finality of death.

The mantra is addressed to Lord Shiva and is also called as Tryambakam Mantra, since Lord Shiva is also called as "Tryambakam" by his devotees. The literal meaning of "Tryambakam" is "the three-eyed one" since Lord Shiva is considered to have a third eye (of destruction).

Mantra: Om Trayambakam Yajamahe,

Sugandhim Pushti Vardhanam,

Urvarukmiv Bandhanat,

Mrityurmokshaya Mamratat

Pronunciation: *Aum Trah-yam-bakam Yaa-jaa-mahey*

Su-gaan-dheem Poo-sh-tee Vaar-dhaa-nam

Ur-vaa-rook-meev Ba-an-dha-nat

M-ree-t-yu-moo-k-sha-yah Maa-m-ra-tat

The closest translation of the hymn would be close to "We worship you – the three-eyed god, who is immortal and who nurtures every being in this world. We honor you and would like to be strengthened. Liberate us from death and everything that is mortal."

When chanted with sincerity, it can help you eradicate even terminal diseases, which denotes the power of this sacred mantra. After attaining a long and healthy life, move ahead and learn how to gain wealth and prosperity in your life using mantras in our next section.

Chapter 6 – Mantras For Wealth & Prosperity

We all like to live a prosperous life. If you lack contentment and happiness in your life, then you would never be able to break the vicious cycle of life and death. There are plenty of mantras in Hinduism that can help you gain wealth, so that you can live a prosperous life. Dedicated to different deities, these mantras have their own distinctive meaning.

Ganesha Mantra

Lord Ganesha is the son of Lord Shivaya. He is considered as the god of prosperity and wisdom in Hindu mythology. It is also believed that before commencing anything significant, if you preach Lord Ganesha, then you won't face any obstacle in between. Try to start your morning by chanting the Ganesha Mantra for a trouble-free day.

Mantra: Om Gam Ganpataye Namo Namah

Pronunciation: Aum Ga-mh Ga-an-paa-ta-yeah Na-moh Na-ma- ha

The mantra invokes the power of Lord Ganesha. It lets you surrender your soul to him while obtaining his blessing. The beloved elephant god can definitely help you eradicate every kind of trouble from your life.

Additionally, you can try the Maha Ganesha Mantra as well – *"Om shreem hreem kreem gloum gam ganapatye varavarada saravajanam me vashamaanaya swaahaa."*

It closely translates to "Oh Lord Ganesha, let all the people in this world live a long and prosperous life by getting your blessings."

Lokah Samastah Mantra

This universal mantra is all about getting empowered. One of the most significant aspects about this mantra is the sense of selflessness that is posses. It is also known as the mantra of universal happiness.

Mantra: *Om Lokah Samastah Sukhino Bhavantu*

Pronunciation: *Aum Lo-kah Sam-ash-tah Soo-k-hee-noh Bha-vaan-tu*

It translates to "May all the beings of this planet be free and happy. May my thoughts, actions, and words contribute in some or other way to bring happiness and freedom to all."

Lakshmi Mantra

Goddess Lakshmi (the wife of Lord Vishnu) is associated with power and prosperity. She is considered to bring wealth and riches in one's life. If you chant the Lakshmi Mantra (also known as Maha Lakshmi Mantra at times), then you would never face any financial problems in your life.

There are different versions and renditions of the Maha Lakshmi Mantra. We have listed some of the most evident mantras of them here.

Mantra: *Om Shring Shriye Namah*

Pronunciation: *Aum Shree-eing Shree-aiye Na-ma-ha*

Mantra: *Om Shreem Maha Lakshmiyei Namaha*

Pronunciation: *Aum Shree-aem Ma-ha Laa-k-sh-mee-yah Na-ma-ha*

Mantra: *Om Sarvabaadhaa Vinirmukto, Dhan Dhaanyah Sutaanvitah, Manushyo Matprasaaden Bhavishyati Na Sanshayah Om*

Pronunciation: *Aum Sar-vah-baad-hah Vee-neer-muk-toh, D-han D-haan-yah Soo-t-aan-vee-tah Maa-nu-sh-yau Maa-t-pra-saa-dien Bh-aa-vee-sh-yaa-tie Na Saa-n-sha-yah Aum*

Mantra: *Om Hreem Shreem Kreem Maha Lakshmi Namaha*

Pronunciation: *Aum H-reem Sh-reem K-reem Ma-ha Laa-k-sh-mee Na-ma-ha*

Chant either one of these mantras every day for a lifetime of wealth, abundance, and fortune.

Padma Lakshmi Mantra

While the Maha Lakshmi Mantra will help you to gain wealth, it is also of utmost importance that you sustain it is as well. Padma closely translates to "being rested", as the mantra will let you preach goddess Lakshmi while she is resting on a lotus.

It is considered that goddess Lakshmi rests on a lotus, which is associated with her purity and divinity. If you want to sustain wealth and good fortune, then chant this mantra every day.

Mantra: *Om Hreem Padmayai Swaha*

Pronunciation: *Aum H-reem Padh-maa-ya S-wa-ha*

Chanting this mantra 108 times using a mala is recommended for optimal results. We are confident that, following this practice, you will find resolutions to all your wealth and financial concerns.

Kuber Mantra

If you are having some financial trouble, then you can resolve it all by chanting the famous Kuber mantra. Kuber is another important deity who is considered as the god of wealth. He also holds a significant place in other religions like Buddhism and Jainism. Just like the Lakshmi mantra, there are different kinds of Kuber mantras as well. Here are some of the most powerful Kuber mantras that you can chant every day.

Mantra: *Om Shreem Hreem Kreem Shreem Kreem Vitteshvaraya Namah*

Pronunciation: *Aum S-hreem H-reem K-reem S-hreem K-reem Veet-tesh-vaa-raya Na-ma-ha*

Mantra: Om Yakshaya Kuberaya Vaishravanaya Dhanadhanyadhipataye

Dhanadhanyasamriddhim Me Dehi Dapaya Svaha

Pronunciation: Aum Ya-k-sha-yah Koo-be-ra-yah Vai-sha-ra-va-na-ya Dha-ana-dh-anya-dhie-pa-ta-ye

Dha-ana-dh-anya-saa-m-ried-dh-eim M-ei D-e-hei Da-pa-ya Sw-a-ha

You can chant these mantras either at the time of sunrise or in the evening as well.

Kuber Lakshmi Mantras

As stated, both Lord Kuber and Goddess Lakshmi are associated with wealth and money. There are some powerful mantras that have combined both these deities together. You can chant either one of these mantras every day to preach both, Lord Kuber and Goddess Lakshmi.

Mantra: Om Hreem Shreem Kreem Shreem Kuberaya Ashta-Lakshmi

Mama Grihe Dhanam Puraya Puraya Namah

Pronunciation: Aum H-reem Sh-reem K-reem Sh-reem Koo-be-ra-ya Aa-sh-tha Lak-sh-mi

Ma-mah G-rei-he Dha-an-am Poo-raa-yah Poo-raa-yah Na-ma-ha

Mantra: Om Shreem Kreem Om Kuber Lakshmi Kamala

Devnaya Dhan Karshinyae Swaha

Pronunciation: Aum Sh-reem K-reem Aum Koo-berr Lak-sh-mi Ka-ma-la

Dev-na-ya Dha-an Kar-shien-ya-ae Sw-a-ha

We are sure that after chanting these powerful mantras, you would be able to move past every trouble related to your wealth and finances. Not only will you attain fortune and prosperity, but you would also be able to create a better tomorrow. If you still have any doubts or fears that you like to conquer, then move ahead to the next chapter, in which we will let you find eternal bliss and peace.

Chapter 7 – Mantras To Attain Peace & Tranquility

If you don't have mental stability and peace in your life, then there is no benefit of having a healthy body or a wealthy lifestyle. Too many times, even after having everything we need, we are not able to cherish all that beauty and joy that the world has to offer.

There are times when we are just afraid to take a leap of faith or when we are not able to move past a bad relationship. This might surprise you, but there are dedicated mantras in Hinduism that can help you attain a perfect balance in your life.

Not just to gain a sense of tranquility, but these mantras can help you overcome your fears or attain a healthy relationship with your loved ones. Let's explore these powerful mantras in detail.

Durga Mantra

Goddess Durga is one of the most powerful female deities in Hindu mythology. She is often called as "Maa" or "the mother" by her devotees. There are nine major incarnations of her, each possessing a distinctive characteristic. It is considered that Goddess Durga was originated from Lord Shiva's left side to slay every evil spirit in the universe.

By chanting the *Durga* mantra, you can easily overcome all your fears and invoke the power of Goddess Durga in you.

Mantra: Sarva Swarupe Sarveshe, Sarva Shakti Samanvite

Bhaye Bhyastraahi No Devi, Durge Devi Namostute

Pronunciation: Saar-vah Swa-roo-pah Saar-veh-she, Saar-vah Sha-akhti Sa-am-an-vi-the

Bha-yeh Bh-yas-tra-ahi N-auh De-vhi, Dur-geh De-vhi Na-am-aus-tu-te

The literal meaning of the mantra is "Goddess Durga, you exist in everything and have infinite power. Please protect me from every kind of fear and adversity."

Kama Deva Mantra

If you are encountering difficulties in your love life, this mantra could be ideal for you. Kama Deva is the God of love, and chanting this mantra invites his blessings. The root sounds "Kleem" or "Kreem" are associated with the energies of love and affection. Begin by chanting this sound 108 times. Subsequently, you can proceed to chant the following *Kama Deva* Mantra.

Mantra: Om Kaam Devaay Vidmahe, Pushpabaanaay Dheemahi, Tanno Ananga Prachodayat

Pronunciation: Aum Ka-am Dev-a-yah Vee-dh-ma-he, Po-sh-pa-ba-na-ay Dh-ee-ma-hie, Taa-n-no Ana-n-gah Pra-a-cha-dhau-ya-at

If you decide to say this mantra ten thousand times across 11 days, you're likely to see some really positive changes. Or, saying it 108 times as the sun sets or during the evening can also make it work really well. If you're feeling lonely and stuck, or if you're having issues with family, using this mantra in the way you prefer can help you find love or sort out problems. Chanting these sacred words can truly bless your life with love and connection.

Pavamana Mantra

If you want to move past the everyday materialistic ideology, then this is just the right mantra for you. The mantra will help you attain tranquility by enlightening your soul.

Mantra: Om Asato Maa Sad Gamaya

Tamaso Maa Jyotir Gamaya

Mrtyor Maa Amrtam Gamaya

Om Shaantih Shaantih Shaantih

Pronunciation: Aum Aa-sah-toh Maa Sa-ad Ga-ma-ya

Ta-ma-soh Maa Jyau-tir Ga-ma-ya

Mra-ta-yor Maa Aam-ra-tam Gam-ma-ya

Aum Sha-an-tih Sha-an-tih Sha-an-tih

The mantra translates to "O Lord, Release me from every realm of unreality or anything which in connecting me to this unreal world. Lead me towards my eternal self and show me what is real."

Also, if you want to take the path of self-realization, then prefer chanting the phrase *"Soham"*. It is translated to "I'm that" and is pronounced as "Soo-ha-aam". It is considered as one of the most thought-provoking mantras and will help you identify who you truly are.

Vaastupurushaaya Mantra

If you are facing any kind of trouble in your family, then you should definitely recite this mantra. It will create a positive aura around your home and will eradicate any unexpected domestic trouble.

Mantra: Om Vaastupurushaaya Namah

Pronunciation: *Aum Va-as-tu-pu-ru-sha-aya Na-ma-ha*

The mantra can also be chanted by you and your spouse (or any other family member) together to create a serene and content environment in your home.

Brahma Mantra

Brahma mantra is considered as one of the most powerful mantras in the Hindu mythology. The mantra can help you attain an overall balance in your life. It is dedicated to Lord Brahma, who is one of the major deities in Hinduism.

From helping you achieve your goals to attaining a healthy environment, the mantra can help you to excel in every sphere of your life. It is often considered that this authentic mantra has the power to fulfill every kind of desire that you might have.

Mantra: Om Eim Hrim Shrim Klim Sauh Sat Chid Ekam Brahma

Pronunciation: Aum E-reem H-reem Sh-reem K-reem S-auh S-at Ch-eed E-kam Brah-ma

The daily chanting of this mantra will ward off every evil spirit and impart a sense of joy and happiness to your life.

Go ahead and try some of these powerful mantras. We are sure they will bring a much-needed change in your life and will liberate you from every kind of negative energy.

Conclusion

Congratulations for finishing this guide so soon! We are sure you must have had a great time attaining an in-depth knowledge about these magical mantras and sacred sounds.

The universe is full of positivity – all you need to do is simply ask. It is really as simple as that!

With the help of these powerful mantras, you would be able to channel your energy and ask for every vital thing that you need from the universe. From health to prosperity and wealth to serenity, you don't need to miss out on anything at all.

Yes! As hard as it might sound – you can have it all. To make things easier for you, we have segregated this guide into different parts. We have provided distinctive chapters, so that you can chant mantras related to your needs.

Additionally, we have walked an extra mile to teach our readers the right way to chant. Most of the beginners make this rookie mistake. Learn how to sit in the correct posture and take our assistance to get it started without making any mistake.

Go ahead and pick some of the most powerful mantras from this guide and start chanting. We are sure you would be able to change your life after being enlightened. You would certainly be able to be a little closer to the universe and reveal your inner self.

Have a great journey exploring yourself!

Namaste.

Printed in Great Britain
by Amazon